# Where does our rubbish go?



Who collects our rubbish? 2
What do people throw away? 3
What can we recycle? 4
Why should we recycle? 6
Where can we recycle? 8
**Story:** Let's Recycle! 9
**Activities** 25
**Picture Dictionary** 30

*Written by Mark Ormerod*
*Illustrated by James Hart*

## Who collects our rubbish?

Here comes the dustcart.

ISLINGTON
Enterprise
10483
This truck has two sections.
This side for your recycling
– the other side for your food and garden waste.
recycle now

And here are the dustmen.

I collect your rubbish.

## What do people throw away?

Many people throw away all these things. Look!

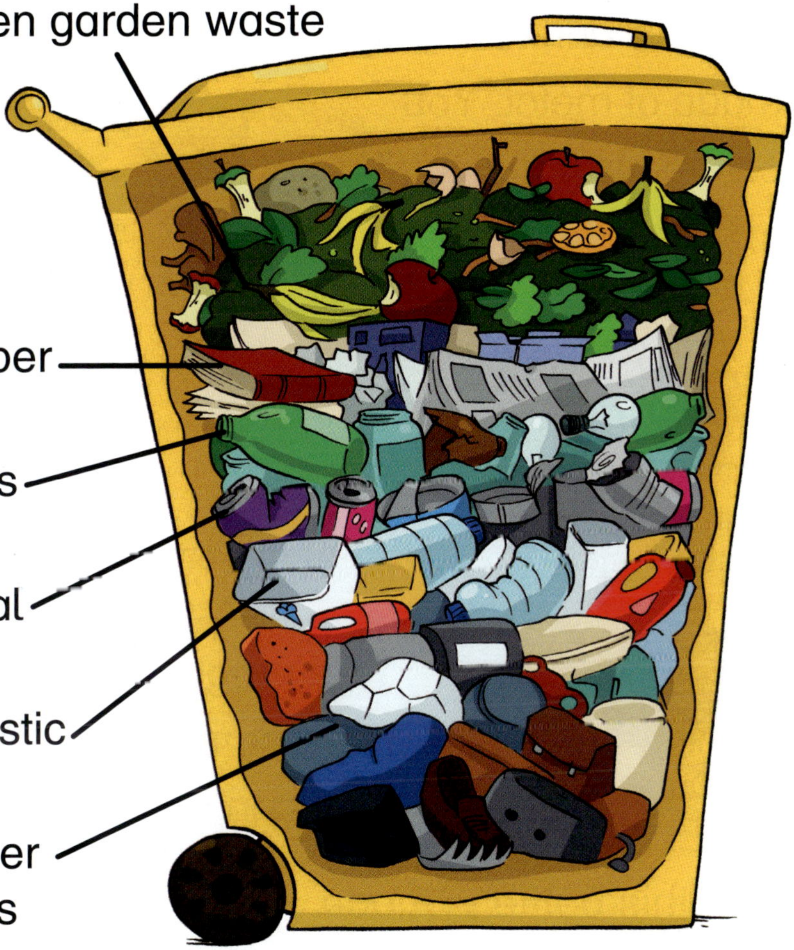


You can recycle most of the rubbish in this bin.

# What can we recycle?

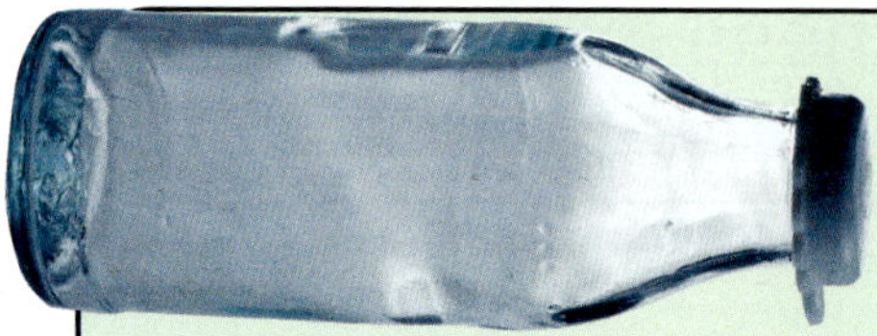

This bottle is made of glass. You can recycle glass.

And this drinks can is made of metal. You can recycle metal.

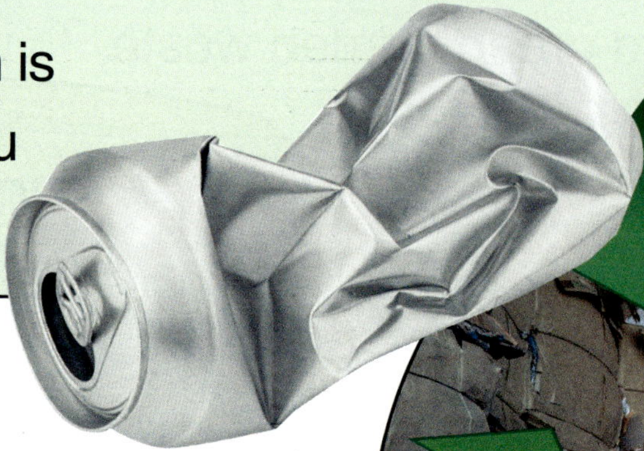

BBC
Wildlife
MAGAZINE
It's a loud world
How our noise confuses and abuses wildlife
How to...
Prepare your garden for winter
Identify wildlife feeding signs
Treat snake bites
Discover Taiwan
Top wildlife hotspots on the beautiful island
The riddle of the panda
The mystery of its bear ancestry
PLUS WIN A £2,300 SAFARI TO KENYA

This magazine is made of paper. You can recycle paper.

And this bottle is made of plastic. You can recycle plastic.

Factories can make new bottles from recycled glass. They can make new drinks cans from recycled metal.

Factories can make notepads from recycled paper. They can make lots of different things from recycled plastic, like rulers and pencil cases.

# Why should we recycle?

Trees, oil, rocks and minerals are natural resources.

1 We make bottles, drinks cans and magazines from plastic, glass, metal and paper.

4 The factory recycles old glass, metal, plastic and paper.

It is important to recycle.

We use natural resources to make glass, metal, plastic and paper.

2 People put old bottles, drinks cans and magazines in the recycling containers.

3 The lorry collects the rubbish and takes it to the factory.

Recycling saves our natural resources.

## Where can we recycle?

Recycling bins are everywhere. You can find them in the streets, in parks and in schools.

Look for the recycling bins near you. Start recycling.
Save our natural resources. Recycle your rubbish!

Recycling Point
Plastic bottles only
Newspapers & Magazines only
Glass bottles only
Drinks cans only

Let's
Recycle!

Written by Mark Ormerod
Illustrated by James Hart

Jilly and Jake live by the sea.

Look, Jilly! It's sunny.
Let's go to the beach.

On the beach, Jilly looks for shells. Jake swims in the sea.

Look! This shell is beautiful.

Later, Jake drinks a can of lemonade and Jilly eats a box of biscuits.

I like lemonade.
I like biscuits.
BISCUITS

Then they throw the drinks can and the empty box in the sea.

The animals are angry with Jilly and Jake.

Don't do that! Don't throw your rubbish in the sea.
Please recycle it!
Put it in a recycling bin.

But Jilly and Jake don't understand.

One day in autumn, it's very windy.

Let's fly my kite.
Okay. Let's go to the river.

The children play by the river. Jake flies his kite and Jilly plays with a boat.

Look at my kite.
Look at my boat.

Later, Jilly drinks a bottle of orange juice and Jake eats a bag of crisps.

Mmm. I love orange juice.
I love crisps.

Then they throw the bottle and the empty bag in the river.

The animals are very angry with Jilly and Jake.

Don't do that! Don't throw your rubbish in the river.
Please recycle it!
Put it in a recycling bin.

But Jilly and Jake don't understand.

One day, in a different part of the world, two children, Anak and Yanouk, are fishing.

Can you see anything?
No, I can't.

Suddenly, the boy is very happy.

Look! Anak, I've got a fish.

But then he is very angry.

It isn't a fish.
It's a plastic bag.

Suddenly, the girl is very happy.

Look! Yanouk, I've got a fish.

But then she is angry.

It isn't a fish.
It's a drinks can.

After fishing all day, the children haven't got any fish. But they've got a lot of rubbish.

Look! I've got nine cans and four bottles.
And I've got seven plastic bags and five boxes.

At home, Anak and Yanouk write a letter.

ENGLISH

The next day, the children give the letter to a snowy owl.

Please give this letter to the children who throw rubbish in the seas and rivers.

Back on the beach, it's a cold but sunny day. Jilly is making a sandcastle. Jake is playing with a ball.

Look at my sandcastle.
Oh no, look at my ball!

Later, the children have a picnic.

Mmm. I love chicken sandwiches.
I love chocolate cake.

As the children finish their picnic, the snowy owl arrives.

Look at this bird, Jake. It's beautiful.
It's got a letter.

Jake opens the letter.

Jilly reads the letter.

Your rubbish is killing
the animals in the sea.
Please recycle your
rubbish. Put it in a
recycling bin.
Anak and Yanouk

Jilly and Jake look at the empty bottles, bags, boxes and cans on the beach.

Let's find some recycling bins.
Good idea.

They put the rubbish in four different recycling bins.

This bin is for recycling glass.
This bin is for recycling paper.

Jilly and Jake recycle all their rubbish.

This bin is for recycling metal.
And this bin is for recycling plastic.

Then the children pick up all the rubbish on the beach. The animals are very happy with Jilly and Jake.

Anak and Yanouk are very happy with Jilly and Jake, too.

Look! I've got a big fish.
This is fantastic! No litter and lots of fish

# Activities

**1 Match the speech bubbles to the recycling bins.**

This bin is for recycling glass.

This bin is for recycling paper.

This bin is for recycling plastic.

This bin is for recycling metal.

**2 Put the letters in order. Write the words.**

1 This rsnkid anc d r i n k s c a n is made of elumt _ _ _ _ _ .

2 This amagzien _ _ _ _ _ _ _ _ is made of rpaep _ _ _ _ _ .

3 This agb _ _ _ is made of pticlas _ _ _ _ _ _ _ .

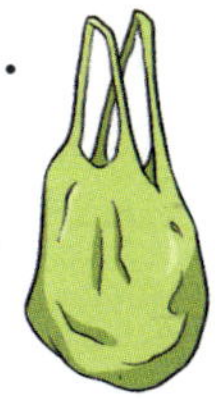

4 This ottble _ _ _ _ _ _ is made of lgsas _ _ _ _ _ .

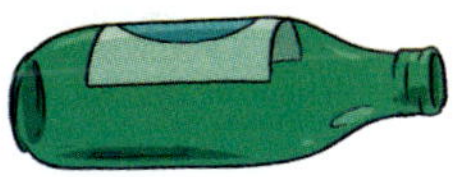

## 3 Label the picture.

| plastic metal paper<br>~~kitchen scraps and green garden waste~~<br>glass other materials |
|---|

1 kitchen scraps and green garden waste

2 ______________________

3 ______________________

4 ______________________

5 ______________________

6 ______________________

## 4 Circle T (True) or F (False).

1 Oil is a natural resource. (T) F

2 Trees and rocks are natural resources. T F

3 Plastic is a natural resource. T F

4 We make paper, plastic, metal and glass from natural resources. T F

5 It is important to recycle to save our natural resources. T F

## 5 Who says it? Match the speech bubbles to the characters.

1 It's a plastic bag.

2 This shell is beautiful.

3 Don't throw your rubbish in the river.

4 Don't throw your rubbish in the sea.

a

b

c

d

## 6 Complete the crossword. Find the secret word.

1 

2 

3 chocolate

3 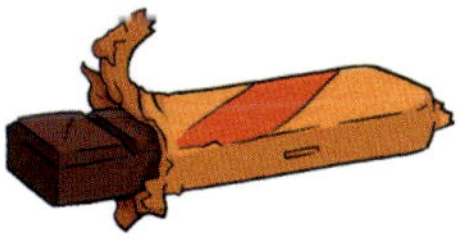

4 

5 

6 

The secret word is _ _ _ _ _ _ .

**7 Match the two halves of each sentence.**

| | | | |
|---|---|---|---|
| 1 | Jake flies | a | in the sea. |
| 2 | Jilly is making | b | for shells. |
| 3 | Jilly looks | c | a letter. |
| 4 | Anak and Yanouk are | d | his kite. |
| 5 | Anak and Yanouk write | e | a sandcastle. |
| 6 | Jake swims | f | fishing. |

**8 Read and complete with the letters *a, e, i, o* and *u*. Colour.**

Y _ _ r r _ bb _ sh _ s k _ ll _ ng
th _ an _ m _ ls _ n th _
s _ _ . Pl _ _ s _ r _ cycl _
y _ _ r r _ bb _ sh. P _ t _ t
_ n _ r _ cycl _ ng b _ n.

Anak and Yanouk

## 9 Complete the crossword.

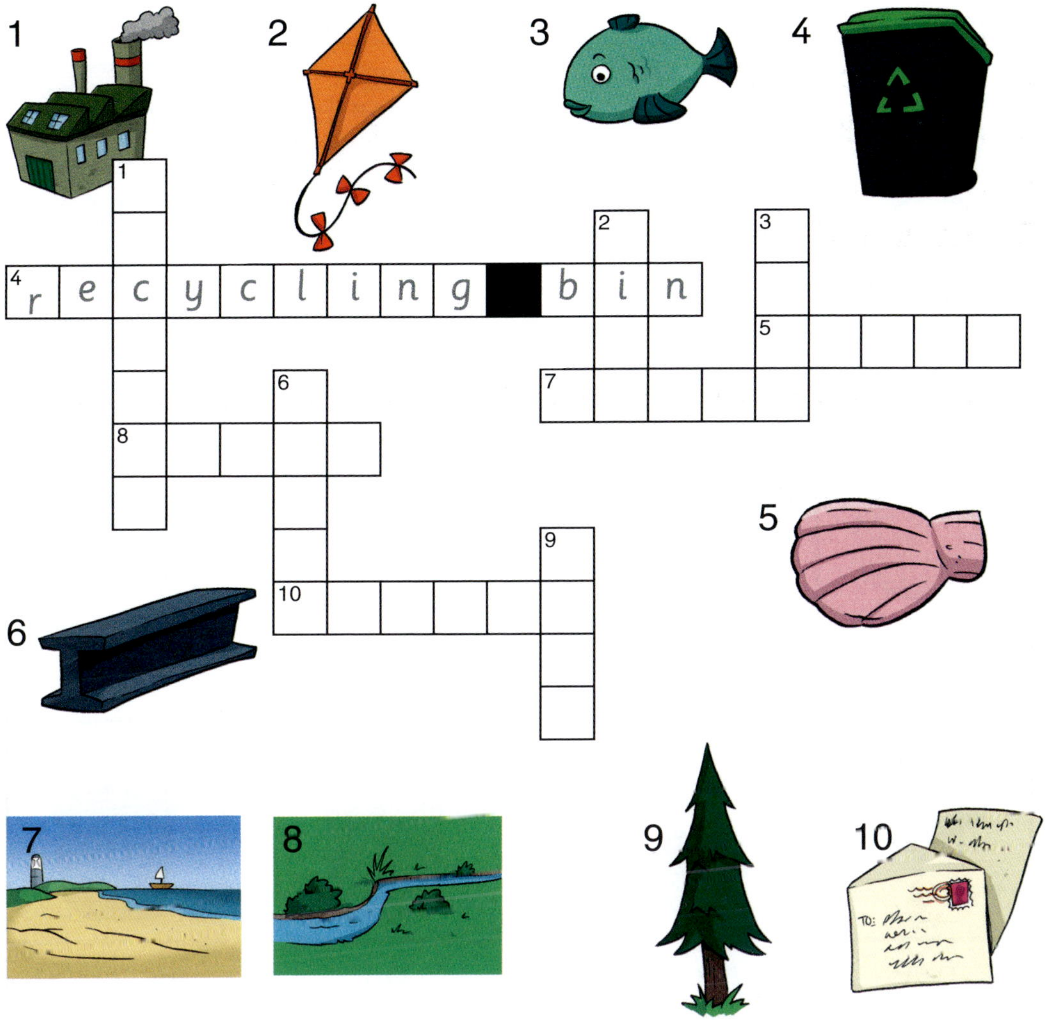

# Picture Dictionary

rubbish

plastic bottle

drinks can

box

bag

glass

metal

paper

tree

rocks and minerals

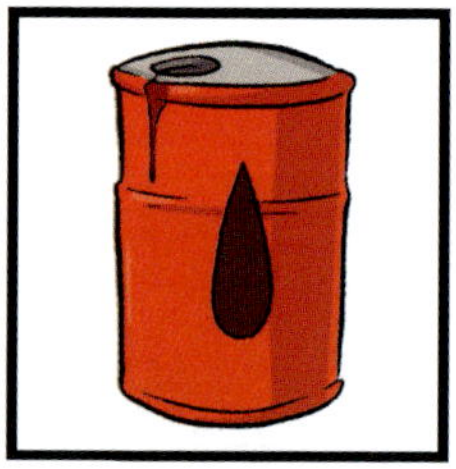

oil

recycling bin

beach

river

windy

sunny

fly a kite

swim in the sea

look for shells

make a sandcastle

boat

ball

fishing rod

snowy owl

chicken sandwich

orange juice

cake

crisps

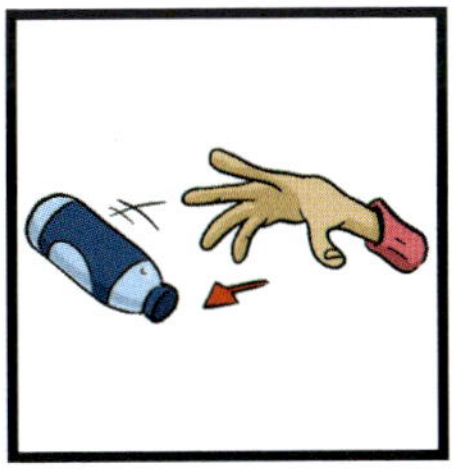
throw

write a letter

angry

happy

Macmillan Education
4 Crinan Street,
London N1 9XW
A division of Springer Nature Limited
Companies and representatives throughout the world

ISBN 978-1-3800-3837-1



First published 2011
This edition published 2019



Illustrated by Peter Harper and James Hart

The author and publishers would like to thank the following for permission to reproduce their photographs:

Cover Photography by Getty Images/Josie Elias.

**Alamy**/Image Anorak p5(t), Alamy/bobo pp4(tl),5(tl), Alamy/A.Hampton Picture Library p7(t), Alamy/Rebrickstock.com p7(b), Alamy/A.Salvemini p4(br), Alamy/P.Tuson p2(t), Alamy Stock Photo/Kzenon p2(b); **Corbis**/P.Thompson p8(b), **Macmillan Education**/ Paul Bricknell p4(bl); **Getty Images**/narvikk p1, Getty Images/Vithun Khamsong p 4 (mr) p5 (ml), Getty Images/iStock/Samokhin Roman p4(tr), **Photolibrary**/F.Roberts p6(b), **Shutterstock**/Africa Studio p5(b).

Picture research Sally Cole/Perseverance Works Ltd.



Printed and bound in Uruguay

2024
14